P9-DTT-421

Clackamas
Community
College

LIBRARY

Oregon City, Oregon

WITHDRAWN

Presented by

Roy F. Sunderland

OLD ENGLISH LUSTRE WARE

John Bedford

WALKER AND COMPANY
NEW YORK

PROPERTY OF
CLACKAMAS COMMUNITY COLLEGE
LIBRARY

© *John Bedford 1965*

All rights reserved. No portion of this work may
be reproduced without permission except for brief
passages for the purposes of review

Library of Congress Catalog Card Number: 66–22379

First published in the United States of America in
1966 by Walker and Company, a division of
Publications Development Corporation

Printed in Great Britain

Contents

Gift (Roy Sunderland)

Introduction

This little book offers an introduction to collecting two kinds of lustre ware.

There is first the traditional English kind—and very English in character most of it is—which once gave an answering gleam to the soft light of candle and lamp in cottage and villa. It appeared in Staffordshire at about the end of the eighteenth century, and has been used ever since for giving china and earthenware a metallic sheen in pinks and purples, silver, gold, and copper. To this type, because of its availability and its very wide range, most of this account is given over.

The other sort, which aims at the 'colour-changing' effects of the prism or the iridescence of the bird's feather, originated much earlier in the Hispano-Moresque wares of the Early Renaissance—and found splendid revival in late-nineteenth-century England.

Collectors of pottery will hardly find a wider choice than in this great ceramic family. Its aristocrats, whether they are the noble heraldic chargers of fifteenth-century Valencia or the charming 'resist' and coloured-ground wares of the English potters, will nowadays call for a deep pocket. On the other hand, the 'bric-à-bracker' in the Portobello Road will find that even now a few pounds patiently and selectively laid out can yield a collection of china which will be hard to beat for variety of texture, shape, colour, and above all the glow of metal.

1. Early Days of Lustre

The story of English lustre ware starts somewhere about the end of the eighteenth century and the beginning of the nineteenth.

Nobody knows quite when the first pieces appeared, nor who made them. There are several claimants to this honour, one of whom speaks for himself. In the year 1846 there appeared in the *Staffordshire Mercury* a letter reading: 'In the notice of the death of Mr John Booth of Well Street, inserted in your last week's paper, it is stated that he was the inventor of lustre for earthenware. I beg to state that this is incorrect as I was the original inventor of lustre, which is recorded in several works on potting, and I first put it in practice at Mr Spode's manufactory for Messrs Daniels and Brown, and continued to make it long before Mr Booth or any other person attempted to do so.'

This letter was signed 'John Hancock, Etruria', a well-known painter and decorator of china and earthenware. He was born in Nottingham in 1758, but his father was a Derby man and apprenticed him to the first William Duesbury, who at that time was as powerful a figure in the world of porcelain as Josiah Wedgwood was in earthenware. Duesbury owned the Derby porcelain works from 1756 to 1786, and bought up Bow (and possibly Longton Hall) in 1760, and Chelsea in 1770. Under Duesbury—who himself had started life as an independent decorator rather than a potter—John Hancock learned the craft of painting and decorating on the fine Derby bodies.

One next hears of him about 1785–6, as an employee of William and John Turner of Lane End, sons of that John Turner who was one of Wedgwood's great rivals. Simeon Shaw says he introduced there the art of gilding china with burnished gold: i.e., applying the metal in a liquid state instead of in the leaf form.

At the time he claims to have introduced the art of using metallic lustres, he was, as we have seen by his own account, working at 'Mr Spode's manufactory for Messrs Daniels and Brown'. This apparently contradictory statement suggests that in fact he was carrying on his craft as a decorator for an independent firm of outside decorators who worked under contract to Spode, or bought wares from him 'in the white' and either decorated them completely, or added lustre or gilt decoration.

This 'Mr Spode's manufactory' will of course be recognized as the famous firm established by the first Josiah Spode in 1776, which, under two further generations of Josiah Spodes and their successors the Copelands, has existed down to the present day. No pieces from these early days seem to have survived. Perhaps Hancock's methods, as is the case with so many ceramic innovators, were too costly for commercial use.

From 1816 until his retirement he was employed at Etruria by Josiah Wedgwood II, as chief colour-maker and manager of the enamelling department: it is possible, therefore, that he may have had a hand in the making of some of the early Wedgwood lustre wares.

'All-over' silver lustre bust of Minerva, c. 1810.

(Opposite) *'All-over'* copper lustre candle-stick in the form of a winged sphinx, 8½ ins. high. (Sotheby & Co.)

Several other names have been offered at various times as the originator of lustre decoration in England. There was Richard Horobin (1765–1830), a joiner carpenter and organ-builder, of whom the *Staffordshire Advertiser* for 1830 speaks as 'The reviver of gold lustre on china and earthenware.' John Aynsley (1752–1829), whose obituary notice reads: 'One of the first manufacturers of porcelain in Lane End, and the first lusterer', was primarily a designer, engraver,

and printer of earthenware. He actually seems to have bought his wares 'in the white' from other potters to whom he sold transfers for use on their own pottery.

Simeon Shaw, author of *History of the Staffordshire Potteries*, published in 1829, and *Chemistry of Pottery* (1837), mentions a John Hancock, together with William Henning, as the introducers in the year 1823 of gold and copper lustring; and also says that the last-named was responsible for the first productions on a commercial scale, at Wolfe's factory in Stoke-on-Trent.

It certainly now seems that in dating commercial lustre ware of the English metallic type as far back as the 1780s, collectors have been making assumptions not borne out by any serious evidence. For example, one can safely discount the legend that lustred pottery was made in the early eighteenth century at Brislington, Bristol, by the Frank family, who once made delftware there. The pieces found in the river-bed, which gave rise to this theory, have since been identified as wares of the Hispano-Moresque iridescent type, which we shall be discussing later in this book (see page 60).

2. The Lustre Families

Lustre decoration is achieved by applying to the earthen-ware or china body a metallic film, the object being either to obtain iridescence or the colour and sheen of a particular metal.

Gold lustre is produced from gold oxide, and copper lustre either from a modification of the gold formula or from copper oxide. A silver effect comes not from the metal itself, which tarnishes, but from platinum. Pink or purple lustre is made by using 'purple of cassius', a precipitate of gold and tin oxide famous for its use in the great Chinese *famille rose* enamel of the Ming Dynasty and later. There are endless variations in the formulæ, and the colour of the body itself has much to do with the result. So, too, does the skill with which the decorated piece is fired in the kiln.

GOLD AND COPPER

For gold lustres, early recipes show that finely powdered gold was added to *aqua regia*, a solvent made up of muriatic (hypochloric) acid and nitric acid: sometimes a small pro-portion of tin was added. This mixture was then combined with a separately produced amalgam of balsam of sulphur and spirits of turpentine.

This gold lustre appears in different hues, due to variations in the alloy or weight: some say that the light 'guinea gold' colour of some early pieces is due to the fact that the potters used actual guineas. But body colour had much to do with the matter. 'Solid' gold and copper lustres get their rich depth when applied to a red-brown body which has first been given a thin smear glaze. At first the copper or bronze effects were produced by combining gold oxide with copper oxide upon deep-coloured bodies. Later, copper oxide alone was used for the cheaper wares.

(Top)
Sunderland jug with view of Wearmouth Bridge and other prints and verses, decorated with 'splashed' pink lustre. Silver resist jardinière on white ground.

(Middle, left to right)
Moulded jug with silver resist on a white ground.
Copper lustre jug.
Jug with applied decoration, painted with pink lustre.
Pink resist lustre jug on white ground.

(Bottom, left to right)
Flower-pot and stand in pink resist lustre on white ground.
Sporting jug painted in colours with silver resist lustre.
Jug painted in colours in reserved panels with pink lustre decoration.
Sporting jug, silver resist lustre on blue ground.

All Delomosne & Son Ltd.

'Splashed' pink lustre miniature teawares—from a service of fifteen pieces.
(Sotheby & Co.)

'SPLASHED' PINK AND PURPLE

When used on a white body—even without a mixture of tin oxide—gold comes out in tones of pink and purple. These last colours appear in many shades and tones, and sometimes in a 'splashed' or mottled form. The method here is to apply the lustre over the glaze of white wares and, while still wet, to spray it with oil through a tube whose end is covered with fine muslin. In the kiln the oil expands and forms tiny bubbles and splashes. Where white panels are left for painting or printing, these are 'reserved' in the same way as with other pottery.

SILVER FROM PLATINUM

As already indicated, silver lustre is not produced from silver, for the oxide of that metal dulls quickly upon exposure to the atmosphere. Instead, platinum is used, the metal having been discovered in South America in about 1750.

As with the gold, platinum metal was dissolved in *aqua regia* and the solution then mixed with spirits of tar. The metal was actually more costly than gold, but since it could be diluted further it worked out cheaper in the end. On a white body only one coating and one firing were necessary, but with the brown bodies this first single coating gave a greyish tone: the full bright metallic lustre could only be achieved by giving a second coating, this time of platinum oxide.

9

3. Lustre Decoration

How is lustre used from a decorative point of view? It may help here if we try to define the various groups into which the wares fall—they could be roughly classified as follows:

1. Plain or 'all-over' lustring in gold, copper or silver, which tries to copy exactly wares made in those metals.

2. Painting by hand, as with enamels, or with stencils.

3. 'Resist' lustre, where the pattern is shown in white (or some other colour) against a lustre background.

4. Transfer printing with lustre decoration.

5. Moulding in relief, with features either wholly or partly decorated in lustre.

6. Figures, either partly or wholly decorated with lustre.

'ALL-OVER' LUSTRE

The heartiest disagreement exists among lustre-ware collectors about 'all-over' or 'solid' lustre decoration. As already indicated, this comprises a very large class of lustre ware in silver and gold which has no other decoration than the lustre itself, and which quite frankly sets out to imitate the effect of articles made of gold, copper, or silver.

Its detractors object to it on the grounds that since pottery has its own admirable qualities it should not try to pretend that it is something else. Supporters of it, on the other hand, claim that by very reason of its leaning towards its cousins in other materials it offers some of the finest shapes to be found in all pottery.

'All-over' wares owe their origin to the enormous reverence paid to gold and silver plate. At first, those who couldn't afford to buy silver tableware and ornaments satisfied themselves with Sheffield plate, that hardly less attractive and much cheaper substitute, whereby a copper foundation made a little silver go a long way. Later on,

*'All-over' gold creamer, with classical reliefs after the Wedgwood school.
'All-over' silver lustre sugar, with bird handles, following late-eighteenth-
century neo-classical styles.*

Sheffield plate itself was imitated in the form of Britannia
metal (see PEWTER in this series), a kind of pewter without
lead, which in its early days burnished as brightly as any
silver.

But pottery could be produced more cheaply still, and
what is more did not need any attention beyond a light
dusting or washing; so it was obvious that once the potters
had found an efficient method of production, they quickly
joined in the highly profitable business of bringing the
gleam of silver into the dark corners of cottages.

FINE POTTING AND SHAPES

While giving the purists their point about imitativeness, one
wonders if they are not missing something by eschewing
these wares. There is very fine potting among them—also
all the elegance and grace of their period. Cast in moulds
and built up, they come in an infinite variety of patterns,
sometimes fairly elaborate in their relief decoration, sometimes bearing only the beading and fluting of the more
restrained neo-classical styles.

Furthermore, when one sees a gathering of them, one
does not have nearly so strong an impression of imitativeness
as with individual pieces. One realizes that they are never
quite like silver or gold; they have a subtly different look,
and of course a very different feel and texture. The early

'all-over' copper wares are attractive in their way, but from about 1840 there is a variety made from copper oxide which is coarser and with many imperfections in the lustring. 'All-over' effects were also produced in the mottled wares which we shall be discussing in due course.

LUSTRE COMBINATIONS

But for those who prefer the 'all-over' effect to be broken up in some way, there are various compromises. Panels can be reserved, and designs either painted or printed in them. Overglaze enamels can be painted over the lustred ground, either on the flat surface or on raised ornamental mouldings. Similarly, white reliefs after the style of jasper ware can be applied to the lustred ground; and there can be bandings in white or colours.

These varieties are not usually as well potted or designed as the earlier plain 'all-over' ware, which relied entirely on their forms and potting qualities. All the same, there is some charming work here. Since they were no longer trying to emulate silver and gold plate, the insides were usually left in the white.

Harvest jug, transfer printed in black with silver lustre banding. (Tunbridge Wells Municipal Museum)

(Opposite) *Silver 'resist' teapot with fruiting vine pattern: from a service of eighteen pieces.* (Sotheby & Co.)

PAINTING AND STENCILLING

Painting in coloured enamels appears on lustre ware as prolifically as upon any other kind of pottery. Sometimes it is applied directly to the lustred surface, but more often it is in reserved panels, like those on the famous Worcester wares with their coloured grounds. There is also painting with the lustre glaze itself, from the 'primitive' and 'cottage' patterns mentioned on page 23, to more sophisticated formal patterns.

Some of these are to be found in stencilled designs on a white or creamware body. Cut-out paper patterns were pasted on to the already glazed wares and the entire surface then covered with a coating of wax. On removing the cut-outs, the design was left exposed and this was painted with lustre. After washing off the wax the ware could be fired to fix the lustre. The potters used the services of the skilled silhouettists of the period who were well known for their extraordinarily fine work with the scissors.

'RESIST' LUSTRES

In the so-called 'resist' wares one finds an admirable combination of silver or gold lustre with grounds either left in the white or with beautiful ground colours, or perhaps with panels of transfer printing or painting.

'Resist' lustre is, in a way, the opposite of stencilled, for here it is the ground itself rather than the painting which forms the pattern. The piece was given the outline of a decoration with a pencil. These forms were then painted with a solution which would literally 'resist' or reject the metallic lustre. Some give the formula for this solution as a mixture of finely pulverized clay with glycerine or honey—others speak of glue-size, or sugar. At all events it had to be greasy enough to repel the metal solution which was applied to the piece. After painting, a wash in warm water would remove both the greasy solution and the lustre sitting on top of it.

In the early days grounds were usually left in the colour of the body, either white or cream, although sometimes grounds were coloured in by hand—they may be distinguished by the uneven surface. There were also blue grounds put in under the glaze, before firing, as in other forms of earthenware and porcelain, the 'resist' patterning being put on over the glaze.

But the finest grounds, which now provide the collectors' darlings, are those applied as enamels over the glaze. The colours are very fine: they include the famous canary yellow, blue, buff, and rarest of all, a rose which is a quite unmatchable partner for the silver lustre.

TRANSFER PRINTING

Some of the happiest effects in 'resist' lustre are those obtained when it is combined with transfer printing, although this process also stands up in its own right. It is thought to have had its origins at the Battersea enamel works, home of the famous 'Battersea Boxes'.

The full story of transfer printing is told in another book in this series (ALL KINDS OF BOXES) but it may be summarized here. The design is engraved on a copper plate, from which prints are taken on paper: these paper prints are then pressed on to the ware—just as children press coloured transfers on to their hands—and the impression is then protected by a glaze. This printing could be in black, blue and other colours, and might be printed over or under the glaze.

FIGURE MODELLING

Almost as much difference of opinion exists about 'all-over' lustre figures as 'all-over' wares generally. Some hold that the unrelieved metallic sheen is a handicap to good ceramic modelling, and certainly the subtle play of light and shade upon colour, which is such an attractive feature of enamelled porcelain and pottery, is lost. These pieces can, of course, be equated in some ways with similar work in black basaltes, or even bronze, and there is admittedly some good potting here. 'The Prussian Hussar' in the British Museum is

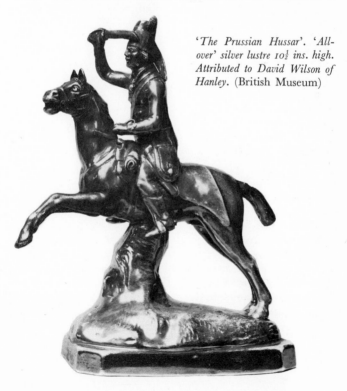

'The Prussian Hussar'. 'All-over' silver lustre $10\frac{1}{2}$ *ins. high. Attributed to David Wilson of Hanley.* (British Museum)

Copper lustre jug with white reliefs in the manner of jasper ware. Maker, Wood & Caldwell, impressed.

as impressive a piece of pottery modelling as you will find anywhere: and it would be an interesting exercise in æsthetic judgement to put this alongside the early salt-glaze or coloured earthenware of Astbury-Whieldon type upon which it was based. One imagines the earlier version would win hands down.

When pink or purple lustre is used 'all-over', as, for example, in the famous cow milk-jugs (see page 53), an element of fantasy creeps in and makes the process more acceptable.

RELIEF OR SPRIGGED WARE

Lustre decoration is also used, however, to decorate figures rather in the same way as the reliefs, for painting features. Some of these efforts are very successful, and form one of the most interesting sub-departments of lustre-ware collecting.

A very wide range of lustre ware makes use of raised, moulded, or sprigged decoration. As already noted under 'all-over' wares, this can take the form of white or other colour reliefs set against a background of lustre, rather in the manner of Wedgwood jasper ware reliefs. Wilson of Hanley is said to have put out lustre ware bearing ivory-white ornament in relief on a blue ground, perhaps in competition with these famous and popular wares. Some of the work was hand-done with delicate tooling, but from say 1820, most of the reliefs seem to have been cast in moulds on coloured bands, alternating with the lustre. Pieces so decorated include those jugs and other ware with continuous scenic bands, perhaps of hunting scenes or teams of horses. These might be coloured with enamels or purple lustre.

Two kinds of lustre could also be used on this raised or sprigged ware, the ground tint being pinkish and the raised ornament of a bronze colour. This was often used with the conventional and very popular grapes and vine leaves. There are also relief figures in coloured enamels of green, yellow, and brown, with the faces in flesh tones.

CHINA AND EARTHENWARE BODIES

It may be helpful at this stage, for those new to china collecting, to say something about the various bodies used.

English porcelain of the eighteenth century—the wares we now revere as the products of Chelsea, Bow, Lowestoft, Derby, Worcester, etc., was not at all the same thing as the 'hard-paste' or true porcelain as made in China for centuries, and also from about 1710 at Meissen (Dresden), when the Chinese secret was rediscovered by Johann Friedrich Böttger, the young German alchemist.

The secret consisted of using two forms of felspathic rock fired at very high temperatures, but not being aware of this,

Ewer with Bacchanalian relief mouldings, painted in enamels and purple lustre. (Victoria & Albert Museum)

17

most of the English potters (like the continental factories at first) made their wares in what is called a 'soft-paste' porcelain, using such materials as clay, lime, soapstone, and other items mixed with ground glass. It was actually a beautiful material in its own right, and preferred by many to the more efficient and brilliant continental product: but it was fragile, delicate, and not at all suitable for those potters who wanted to compete with the European product in their own market—which many of the larger potters did. They also had their own rapidly expanding market for tea-wares which would look as decorative as the expensive goods from Derby and Worcester, but would stand up to hard wear.

CHAMPION'S HARD-PASTE

One exception to the general run of soft-pastes made in the eighteenth century in England was a hard-paste or true porcelain made first at Plymouth between 1770 and 1781 by William Cookworthy, the Plymouth Quaker chemist who, fifty years after the German Böttger, independently discovered the Chinese secret all over again, using Cornish china clay and china stone. His patent was bought by Richard Champion, who worked it for a time but eventually sold out to a consortium of Staffordshire potters, including such well-known ones as Samuel Hollins, Jacob Warburton, and John Turner. They took over the New Hall at Shelton, and made there hard-paste porcelain under Champion's patent—the first 'true porcelain' ever made in Staffordshire.

ENGLISH BONE CHINA

The hard-paste produced at New Hall, however, was never destined to take over as the main body for English ceramic wares, as had happened on the Continent. Instead, some of the leading potters started to experiment with a mix which made a great deal more use of bone ash—there had always been a little of this in most of the English wares—and by the early nineteenth century most of the leading factories had moved over to what was now called bone china. Even New Hall produced a version of it alongside their hard-paste porcelain.

SEMI-PORCELAIN OR IRONSTONE

This is the body used for a great deal of the better class of lustre ware. It was also used on some of the tougher sorts of earthenware introduced to compete with the bone china and Chinese porcelains. It was variously called stone china, semi-porcelain, etc., the most celebrated being the famous Mason's Ironstone, a practically indestructible ware usually decorated with showy patterns modelled on Chinese and Japanese motifs.

COMPARING BODIES

The lustre seeker, in familiarizing himself with these various bodies—which he will need to do if he takes his collecting at all seriously—will find it useful to compare identified pieces of pottery of all kinds. I do not know of any soft-paste porcelain with lustre decoration, so one should start by getting to know the early bone chinas of, for example, Josiah Spode, and the bodies used by Mintons, Davenport, and other Staffordshire men of the early days.

Jug moulded with horizontal grooves, coloured alternately in cream colour and pink lustre. (Sotheby & Co.)

The various sorts of earthenware are a study in themselves, from the heavy stone chinas just mentioned to the extremely light and tender bodies used before the middle of the century, with their distinctive glazes. These have nothing like the highly efficient finishes produced towards the end of the century: they have a shimmery look when viewed at an angle, and the larger plates and other pieces often have three little rough marks round the rim. These are the marks left by the cockspurs which the potters used to keep the plates from sticking together when they were being fired in the kiln.

To find one's way around these various bodies is not nearly so difficult as it sounds. After frequent handling, one soon gets used to the 'feel' of them, and can put them in a period without much difficulty. The 'feeling' can be done in shops—providing one doesn't wear out one's welcome. But it can also be done in the better sale-rooms where not only are the goods put out in cabinets for inspection, but often the cataloguer is prepared to go out on a limb and let you have the benefit of his guesses. 'Probably Spode' can mean something—in the right catalogue.

4. Things Made in Lustre Ware

What articles were made in lustre ware? The simple answer to this seems to be to point to almost everything made in all other kinds of earthenware and china. Looked at in one way, lustring is simply a method of decorating ceramics, and those who used the process were usually makers of wares decorated in all kinds of ways. For this reason, of course, the collector will often find himself treading on the heels of other specialists, and perhaps being robbed of his quarry because it has some point of interest or rarity on different grounds, as might be the case with a figure by Ralph Salt or Enoch Wood.

This will be no handicap: in fact it should be a great help in identifying finds, for much lustre ware is unmarked—perhaps a greater proportion than of any other kind of ware. Why this should be so is something of a mystery. It is true that many of the wares are of comparatively low quality, and the potters making these as well as better-class articles would perhaps not like to associate their names with these cheaper wares. But there is lustre—such as some of the magnificent silver 'resist' wares with coloured grounds— which can bear comparison with anything being made at the time. Very little even of this is marked.

So the collector who extends his studies into other men's fields may well find points of correspondence which will be of the greatest help to him. Instances of this are given in the section on Swansea lustre (see page 47).

There are special departments of ceramics where lustre plays a much larger part than other forms of decoration, and even some, like the Sunderland 'splashed' ware, where it takes over the lion's share of the collector's attention. We shall be looking at some of these as we go along.

So far as sheer quantity is concerned, of course, the biggest department of lustre ware now available to the collecting public consists of tea and table wares. If one includes here the jugs and mugs, this was probably always the most prolific branch of production so far as numbers of pieces is concerned.

Of these, the shops today most often offer cups and saucers separately, more rarely united. Nowadays there seem always to be more odd cups than odd saucers. This may partly be due to the fact that an original set may have been combined with coffee cups, and so started life with only half as many saucers as cups: it is more likely that odd saucers which have lost their cups have been more eagerly bought than odd cups—their usefulness as ashtrays or as pickle plates is obvious.

All the same, if one is going in for lustre ware determined to make a show, it is well worth while picking up these odd items. Many of the patterns are identical or strongly similar, even though they have been made in quite different centres, and it is surprising how often one is able to match up pieces. More rarely there are sets or part sets which are worth buying as a basis and adding to as opportunity offers. And here again some general knowledge of shapes and styles will help to suggest what kind of teapot should be sought for a given type of jug or sucrier.

COTTAGES AND CHURCHES

Most often met with among the teawares, perhaps, are those with sometimes very crudely painted views of houses, cottages, or churches. It was Mr Atwood Thorne who in the early 1920s seems first to have given these simple but far from unattractive wares the dignity of an appearance in his book on lustre ware, *Pink Lustre Pottery*. Until then collectors were usually interested only in grander varieties like 'resist' and the rest. Not being any kind of lustre-ware collector to begin with, Mr Thorne bought a lustre-ware teapot of this

*Plate with wicker and green basket weave border (see page 53) with a
'house' pattern in pink lustre. 8 ins. diameter. Presumably Swansea.
(Sotheby & Co.)*

sort merely because it reminded him of taking tea at his
grandmother's. Not only was he content to snap up such
unconsidered trifles but it mattered nothing to him that the
teapot lacked a lid—which he matched up in due course.

What he called the 'cottage' design shows a house or
cottage, more or less sketchily drawn, with trees, a fence,
and a border. The 'primitive' variety, however, is even more
sketchy—it also shows a house, or a church, or perhaps a
castle, but the drawing is primitive indeed, consisting of not
much more than a few lines. In fact, as Mr Thorne pointed
out, they look exactly like the sort of drawings one made as
a child, and which are still being made by one's own children
and grandchildren.

These designs are found on pieces from very widely
different sources, and it seems obvious that they are the sort
of journeyman work which anyone, perhaps women, girls,
or even children, was expected to be able to do for a few
pence the dozen. But there is something in their very crudity
which makes a gathering of them attractive on one's shelves.

'All-over' silver Toby teapot.
(Castle Museum, Norwich)

STRAWBERRY PATTERN

More careful versions of these are to be found in pink lustre, and also in other colours where the lustre is used for a border. But an entirely different class of painting, more comparable with that on other decorated wares, is to be found usually on better-class bone china. Outstanding is what collectors call the strawberry pattern, with the fruit in red, hulls and leaves in green, and tendrils in pink. Mintons, and also Swansea and New Hall, were among those who used this pattern. A set usually comprised six cups and saucers, teapot, creamer, sucrier, and slop-basin.

Of the same kind, and similarly varied, are all the mugs —some say that there were small tea-sets which provided a cup and saucer for every little girl and a mug for every little boy. From here it is only a step to the joking mug which as you drink, reveals to your horrified eyes a frog lurking on the bottom. Sometimes these are so contrived that as the last drops of liquid pass under his legs there is a frightful

One of a pair of pink lustre furniture stops in the form of lions. (Sotheby & Co.)

24

Bull in brown or copper lustre, probably by Dawson & Co., Sunderland.
(Sunderland Museum)

gurgling sound, as though the creature was alive and ready to jump. The race of lustre also includes its puzzle jugs with secret passages which you must stop up if you want to drink without drenching yourself.

JUGS AND PLAQUES

Jugs are here in enormous variety, from those in mottled pink with verses, to others where silver combines with splendid colours. Plaques with mottoes or verses, sailing-ships and landscapes within painted frames, were made for Victorian walls. Chimney ornaments of all kinds, especially animals, were offered for the mantelpiece.

There were watch- and clock-stands, rolling-pins for the kitchen or to hang over the fireplace in the kitchen and keep out the bogles; candlesticks for the bedside, carpet balls to play with on the floor during winter evenings. Easter and birthday eggs had their lustre versions. Figures like those seen in other kinds of pottery were made either with lustre 'all-over' or so spotted and touched: sometimes they appear in 'useful' forms like Toby jugs or cow milk-jugs. There are bell-pulls, small furniture stops to keep your spinet from digging its sharp toes into the floor, bough pots, flower

Watch-stand in coloured enamels and pink lustre. Impressed 'Dixon, Austin & Co.', 1820–6. (Sunderland Museum)

holders, pastille burners, water flasks, knife-rests, egg-stands, punch bowls, ewers and basins. There are wine cups, inkpots, water fonts, snuff boxes, stirrup cups; there are even chamber-pots.

SALT, PEPPER—AND TODDY

Salt-cellars may be found and occasionally pepper pots or casters. Collectors of the enviable past also speak of toddy-sets, comprising a bowl for sugar and three pitchers graduated in size, the largest for the revered beverage itself, the next for the contributory hot water, the smallest for port or claret. Pipes and tobacco jars in lustre ware complete the party.

GOBLETS AND LOVE-FEAST CUPS

Much interest attaches to the large race of goblets in lustre ware, sometimes in 'all-over' gold or copper, sometimes with reliefs, or pleasantly coloured overglaze sprigging as found on slipware. There is also blue overglaze floral painting and splashed pink or purple. They come in various forms, some in what glass collectors would call rummer-shape, others bell or ogee or cupped. Some call them funeral goblets, and this seems to be confirmed by inscriptions. 'He that believeth shall be saved' appears on one from the Garrison Pottery, Sunderland; while another from the same place reads: 'For man dieth and wasteth away, yes, man giveth up the ghost and where is he' (Job 14, 10). Another has a portrait of a Wesleyan minister: one wonders in this case if

26

the goblet is one of the communion cups used in smaller places of worship.

There are also marriage cups, or loving cups, with such rhymes as:

> The Lord unite us both in one
> And in his love may we agree,
> To praise him while on earth we live
> That after death may happy be.

Mr J. T. Shaw, of the Sunderland Museum, tells me that they tend to refer to their two-handled cups as 'Love Feast Cups' when they are inscribed with texts and/or portraits of John Wesley, Hugh Bourne, or other religious leaders. But when the names of the two recipients are on the cups they are thought of as marriage cups. At Sunderland, these cups come in two shapes: one is a two-handled goblet form on a stemmed foot (see below); the other two-handled and cylindrical, the body tapering from foot to rim, rather like a two-handled mug.

Mug, goblet, and two-handled loving, love-feast, or marriage cups in various lustre techniques. (Sunderland Museum)

5. Round the Lustre Ware Centres

A. STAFFORDSHIRE

Everyone likes to know, if at all possible, where their finds were made, when, and by whom. As we have seen, lustre ware presents unusual problems in this respect. With so many other wares, the potters proudly stamp or print their marks, inviting the world to buy on the strength of their name and reputation. Here, with a few exceptions, they are usually mute. The suggestion has already been offered that this may be because the larger potters were not particularly proud of their work in lustre ware. But it may also be that some of the smaller potters left their wares unmarked in the hope that they might be taken for the products of one of the more celebrated factories.

COMPARISONS ARE USEFUL

In spite of all these difficulties, one can get some clues by looking at the known work of the various centres. We will often find that exactly the same kind of thing was made at quite different places; but those who are prepared to look very hard at some of these apparently identical things may

Tripod incense burner in red earthenware covered with gold lustre. Wedgwood's, Etruria, dated 1805. Height 5¾ ins.

(Opposite) *Candlestick in earthenware decorated with silver 'resist' lustre. Wedgwood's, Etruria, late eighteenth century.* (Victoria & Albert Museum)

28

find some interesting distinctions. There is hardly a field of ceramics in which so much sifting still needs to be done by the assiduous and interested collector.

In our progress round the potteries we cannot do better than start with the largest centre of all—the collection of villages around Stoke-on-Trent which grew into Arnold Bennett's Five Towns, and which make up the largest centre of pot-making in the world. They are called the Potteries (with a capital P)—as distinct from the Out-Potteries, the collective name for the other areas of production.

'MR SPODE'S MANUFACTORY'

If we accept John Hancock's claim that he was the inventor of lustre decoration, and that he 'first put it into practice at Mr Spode's', then one ought appropriately to start with that famous factory. At what date lustre ware was first decorated there can only be guesswork. Hancock's first employers at Hanley, William and John Turner, went bankrupt in 1806, owing to the loss of their father's trade due to the Napoleonic Wars. Simeon Shaw, the historian of the Potteries who delved into its story in the 1820s, indicates that Hancock was working for the Turners 'for some time prior to 1800'.

Now about this time, the Josiah Spodes, father and son, were engaged in developing the new bodies already mentioned. From about 1790 they marked most of their wares, so that we can identify some of their lustre. Those pieces which have survived seem mostly to have been of the mottled pink type very much like the Wedgwood 'moonlight' wares shortly to be described. There are also jugs and bowls

'Moonlight' lustre wall pocket in the nautilus shape. Wedgwood's, Etruria, 1810. Height 6 ins. (J. Wedgwood & Sons Ltd)

in this mottled pink with reserved bands carrying borders and panels of flowers: these bear the mark SPODE printed in red.

Another Spode contribution is seen in a version of the jugs popular at the time which bear impressed reliefs of sporting and other subjects: in one specimen the deep neck is decorated in solid gold lustre—it bears the mark impressed in the bottom. No silver lustre seems to have been definitely attributed to Spodes—although that, of course, is not to say that some will not appear one day.

WEDGWOOD'S

Contrary to general belief it does not appear that the first Josiah Wedgwood used lustre decoration, but the second Josiah Wedgwood certainly entered the race, for there are marked pieces extant in gold lustre bearing the date 1805. From soon after this date, however, comes the lustre ware with which Wedgwood's are chiefly associated. They called it 'moonlight' lustre, and it was a pink splashed or mottled type with orange-yellow speckling, usually applied to shell forms, such as the nautilus or the pecten. Large services were made in this ware as well as wall pockets, vases, bell-pulls, pastille burners, flower-holders, and other items.

Wedgwood's embarked upon gold and silver lustring, and in view of the founder's preoccupation with classical forms it is not surprising that much of it should have been made in these styles. There is a well-known pastille burner in the Empire style, with inverted dolphins forming a tripod, in the Victoria and Albert Museum, London. In this specimen the gold lustre is applied over brown earthenware, but there are other versions where the body is the famous black basaltes developed by the first Josiah.

'All-over' silver of exceptional brilliance was produced by the firm, especially in coffee- and teawares, also candlesticks and other pieces. They also did some very handsome work in silver 'resist'. Of their work later in the century, and also in the recent past, more will be said in another chapter.

LAKIN AND POOLE

The name of Thomas Lakin occurs in two ways in connexion with early Staffordshire lustre ware. First, there are pieces with paintings of rustic scenes in pink lustre, and also some with the perforated basket edge popular in creamware, which bear the mark LAKIN. Some authorities say that Lakin ceased to work on his own account after 1799, so these pieces may well be among the very earliest lustre ware which has survived. Secondly, his widow in 1824 published his recipe book, *Potting, Enamelling and Glass Staining*, which gives us much of the information we now have about the early processes.

BAILEY AND BATKIN

William Bailey and his partner W. Batkin, and their successors, have left their mark on lustre wares. This firm was principally interested in domestic ware in gold and silver lustre, using the initials 'B & B' as their mark: later, in the 1820s, the firm seems to have lost its Batkin and acquired a Harvey, for the impressed mark with these two names appears on wares with pinkish gold lustre. The lost Batkin seems later to have linked up with a potter named Booth.

One of the very largest of the Staffordshire lustre-ware manufacturers—as they were also one of the largest makers of any kind of pottery—was the firm founded by Enoch Wood, a member of the great potting family headed by the famous figure-maker, Ralph Wood. After being apprenticed to both Josiah Wedgwood and Henry Palmer of Hanley, Enoch Wood set up on his own as a master potter about 1781 at the age of twenty-four. He had shown remarkable skill as a potter even before he was twenty and soon established a thriving business. In 1790 he was joined by James Caldwell of Linley Wood, probably a sleeping partner, and for the next twenty-eight years they built up a very large business in all kinds of Staffordshire wares, from jasper and black basaltes to blue-printed earthenwares. He was chiefly known, however, for his figures which, although without the charm and delicacy of those of Ralph Wood, mark important technical developments and also had a huge sale. The story of this family and its figures is told in another book in this series (STAFFORDSHIRE POTTERY FIGURES).

Enoch Wood decorated some of his figures with lustre, but most of these suffer from the rather tasteless feeling of Wood's own modelling: the firm's work was much more pleasing when they turned to the popular jugs and teawares of their day, of which they must have had a very large output. Various marks were used, from the early WOOD & CALDWELL to E. WOOD & SONS BURSLEM—this last after 1818 when the partnership with Caldwell ended. These jugs show all manner of decorative devices—colour glazes, relief ornament, and the rest, all in combination with fine lustre. Like much of Wood's work they lack final refinement and taste, but they have a strong period flavour and are highly regarded by collectors.

DAVID WILSON AND PETER WARBURTON

Among other Staffordshire firms making lustre ware was that of David Wilson who took over a factory from his

Cupid with bow and arrow and flaming torch. His drapery and wings are in pink lustre. Probably by Wood & Caldwell, Burslem, about 1810–15. (Sotheby & Co.)

brother Robert at Hanley: the latter had been a partner in one of the Palmer and Neale successions—famous makers of earthenware figures. Pieces bearing the impressed mark WILSON generally show 'all-over' lustre on the outside and white inside. Wilson is also credited with inventing a purple lustre, the colour of ripe blackberry juice, which was copied by other potteries. The 'all-over' silver figure of 'The Prussian Hussar' in the British Museum, shown on page 15, has been attributed to him.

The impressed mark WARBURTON stands for Peter Warburton who made creamware at Cobridge, and was a partner in the New Hall Company. In 1810 he took out a patent for printing in 'gold, silver, and platina' with transfers on earthenware and bone china. This seems to have been a kind of bat-printing, whereby the copper plate was oiled instead of being inked, and the design then transferred to the pieces by means of a flexible blue sheet or 'bat', which had been sprinkled with powdered metal. Warburton also made silver 'resist'.

DAVENPORT

John Davenport of Longport, in his day, must have made every kind of ware with every type of decoration, and in almost every body known, from transfer printed wares and heavy ornate 'Japans' to 'New Hall cottage' and mid-Victorian pictorial porcelain. It is therefore no surprise to know that he had a hand also in lustre ware. He marked with the name DAVENPORT, but perhaps there are pieces bearing his well-known anchor.

Ridgeway is another great name in Staffordshire pottery, which is also to be found on lustre ware.

NEW HALL

New Hall is unique not only in introducing hard-paste to Staffordshire (see page 18), but in setting a style of its own which was taken up by a number of potters. In some ways it harked back to the simple classical forms popular in the last two decades of the eighteenth century—there is a famous 'silver shape' teapot. In others it seemed to derive from the pleasant little sprigged designs popular on everyday earthenware: the wares have justly been called 'cottage' porcelain. Still other designs incorporate freely drawn birds and other subjects with an oddly modern feeling.

The porcelain was sometimes marked with pattern numbers preceded by 'N' or 'No' in script: the later rather dull white bone-china body usually had the name of the factory inside a double circle, printed in brown or red. But there is much New Hall ware which is unmarked, and also much from other factories which passes as New Hall in many collections. Marks used on pieces in the New Hall styles include those of Miles Mason, founder of the firm which developed the famous ironstone. The early Minton pattern books also follow them. Outstanding among the lustre wares in this family are pleasantly fresh and simple rustic patterns of birds and landscapes with pink or silver lustre. There are also some formal patterns made up of white lines taken out with a point.

MINTONS

Mintons have been mentioned several times, as they must be in any account of nineteenth-century ceramics. This illustrious firm was founded in 1793 by that Thomas Minton who once worked as an engraver for Thomas Turner of Caughley, and is said to have produced the first willow-pattern design. The early Minton wares were chiefly of earthenware, for although bone china was made from 1798, it was not developed as a major product until about 1825. In the early years they seem to have followed the simple restrained sprig patterns of New Hall types; but later their work in lustre ware appears to have been overshadowed by the great variety of their other decorative schemes, well known to collectors and the general public.

The mark of Charles Allerton and Sons, of Longton, established in 1831, appears on popular wares like Toby jugs and teapots, jugs in 'peasant' floral designs and also some foliate patterns rather like those on Victorian Wedgwood Queensware. The wares made before about 1870 were unmarked.

B. SUNDERLAND

When you use the term 'Sunderland' in the trade today—and even among some collectors—it will be assumed that you are talking of that mottled or 'splashed' type of pink lustre which, as we have already seen, was made in other centres as well. A great deal of it does come from the northeast coast port, so it is little wonder that the name has stuck. One suspects that the famous Sunderland or Wearmouth Bridge, of which we shall be speaking presently, also had a good deal to do with it.

NORTH HYLTON

The earliest important pottery was North Hylton, or Hylton Pot Works as it was first called, established by William Maling, a landowner of Sunderland. In or about 1815 the Maling sons and their successors transferred to the Newcastle area, and the Hylton works came under the control of John Phillips, the manager, or his son. This family already owned the Sunderland or Garrison Pottery, a much larger concern.

The North Hylton factory made a speciality of creamware

'Primitive' pattern jugs and plate, possibly made at the Garrison Pottery, Sunderland. (Sunderland Museum)

mugs commemorating births and marriages, with fine clear hand-lettering. It also made pink lustre pottery. Marks used were MALING (although this has to be distinguished from the work done by this family at Newcastle): JOHN (or J.) PHILLIPS, and HYLTON POTTERY.

These have been noted on pieces printed with the view of Wearmouth Bridge, scenes depicting the Battle of Trafalgar, 'Jack on a Cruise', and 'Ascent of the Aerial Balloon'.

LOW FORD, OR DAWSON'S

In the heyday of lustre ware one of the finest potteries on Wearside was the Low Ford, or Dawson's Pottery, at South Hylton, then known as Ford. It was founded by John Dawson, both of whose sons predeceased him, so that when he died at the age of eighty-eight in 1848, the business fell into the hands of his grandson and gradually disintegrated. But when it was in full spate the firm made high-quality creamware, and such diverse things as earthenware table-tops with pictures of Napoleon's battles, marbles, and other novelties. They also made copper and silver lustre, and tea-wares painted in pink lustre with the 'primitive' and 'cottage' designs.

As already mentioned, these designs were used at many places, but the Dawson's marks on cups and saucers with the pattern traces it to at least one source. These marks were variations on the name Dawson or Ford, or Low Ford Pottery.

SOUTHWICK POTTERY

A long-lived family business was established in 1788 at Southwick—then a small township on the outskirts of Sunderland—by an Anthony Scott who had managed a pottery at Newbottle, one of the very earliest centres of potting in the district. This concern, through successive generations, sometimes with three representatives working at the same time, built up a fine business in all kinds of earthenware, and only came to grief in 1897 because of competition for labour from the ship-building industry.

They had an exceptional variety of wares to their name, but they too joined in the local pink lustre speciality and have left some marked wares with their name in various forms. They can roughly be dated by reference to a table given in the Sunderland Museum's booklet (see page 42).

Sunderland copper lustre of about 1820–30, including a shaving dish with a hole for hanging by a cord. (Sunderland Museum)

It should be noted that the names Scott and Scott Brothers were used by a pottery at Portobello, near Edinburgh, which also made lustre ware.

A link with Swansea is seen in one of the patterns put out by the Wear, or Moor Pottery, Southwick, which was established in 1789 and in 1803 was taken over by Samuel Moore and Peter Austin, trading as S. Moore & Co.: it remained in the hands of the Moore family until 1861. The pattern referred to, which was only one of a great many lustre items produced by the firm, was found on plates with pierced rims and basketwork borders rather like Leeds and Wedgwood creamware, the centres decorated with birds painted in pink lustre. An example in the Sunderland Museum collection is marked 'Moore & Co', while an identical pair in the National Museum of Wales—illustrated by Morton Nance in his colossal work *The Pottery and Porcelain of Swansea and Nantgarw*—are marked 'Dillwyn & Co Swansea'. The question is, who first used the style and who copied it: or is this another case of a painter travelling

about from place to place in search of work? Marks of this pottery are variants on Samuel Moore & Co, Moore & Co, S.M. & Co.

DIXON AND AUSTIN

The well-known mark of Dixon and Austin, sometimes coupled with the name of Phillips, brings us back to that Sunderland or 'Garrison' Pottery established near the barracks at the eastern end of the town, which was taken over by John Phillips of the North Hylton Pottery. From 1828 the firm was variously known as Dixon Austin & Co., and the concern was wound up in 1865 and the transfer plates bought by the Ball Brothers and used in their Deptford (Sunderland) Pottery.

Here were made, among other lustre wares, the well-known chimney ornament dogs with copper lustre spots familiar in Staffordshire; greyhounds, watch- and clock-stands, rolling-pins, and carpet balls, teawares with the 'cottage' pattern, plaques with religious mottoes, 'bridge' views, copper and silver lustre jugs commemorating the marriage of Queen Victoria in 1840, Easter and birthday eggs, and two-handled lustre chamber-pots.

(Far left) *Sunderland pink lustre ewer and basin, with views of Wearmouth Bridge, shipping, etc. Impressed* 'Dixon, Austin & Co', *c. 1816–19.* (Sunderland Museum)

(Left) *Sunderland figures from a set of* 'The Seasons', *in coloured enamels and pink lustre. Marked* 'Dixon, Austin & Co.', *impressed.* (Sotheby & Co.)

39

The only other major pottery in Sunderland district likely to have been engaged in making lustre ware was the Deptford or Ball's Pottery. It was established in 1857 by William Ball, son of a Burslem man who had been trained at Dawson's Low Ford pottery and work continued under his sons down to 1918. They made mainly brown ware and cane ware, but they also imported earthenware from elsewhere, which they decorated with transfer designs from copper plates bought from the Garrison, Moore's, and Scott's, and decorated it with lustre of what the Sunderland Museum booklet calls a decidedly orange colour.

The ware was heavier, whiter and had more 'staring' glaze than the local product, and the printing, most unusually for Wearside, was sometimes done in blue, green, and brown. Where the transfer plates bore the name of the pottery which had originally had them engraved, Ball left

Sunderland jug, printed in black with view of the Wearmouth Bridge, and decorated with pink lustre. Signed, 'J. Phillips Hylton Pottery'. (Victoria & Albert Museum)

this on, thus adding to the painful delights of collectors in seeking attribution. Ball himself claimed that he had every right to do so as his was itself an old Sunderland firm like those defunct ones from whom he had bought the plates. All the same, collectors may perhaps be grateful to the Balls for leaving so many clues behind them, even if they take a little unravelling.

Most of the designs, of course, are similar to those of the other potteries, but there are a few not found on their wares. Among these are 'Agamemnon in a Storm', 'Manchester Oddfellows', and that Jack Crawford who earned imperishable fame on so much pottery by his gesture in nailing the flag to the mast at Camperdown:

> At Camperdown we fought
> And when at worst the fray
> Our mizzen near the top, boys,
> Was fairly shot away.
> The foe thought we had struck,
> But Jack cried out 'Avast'
> And the colours of old England
> He nailed up to the mast.

The firm, with terrific rectitude for once, printed on this design, 'Copyright Ball Brothers, Sunderland'.

WEARMOUTH BRIDGE

Most celebrated of all the designs on Sunderland lustre is the bridge—or rather, two bridges—of which the town was so justly proud. Collectors call it Sunderland Bridge, but its proper name is the Wearmouth Bridge.

The first bridge, in its day, was an engineering prodigy. At its opening, on 9 August 1796, it was the longest single-span cast-iron bridge in the world. Its span was 236 feet, the height from low-water mark 100 feet, and the spring of the arch 33 feet. The bridge had six cast-iron ribs and a width of 32 feet, the superstructure being of timber. Its building was sponsored by that Rowland Burdon, M.P., to whose family the Sunderland Museum owes the fine Rowland Burdon collection of Sunderland lustre pottery.

Pictorially there are really two bridges to consider, for in the year 1858 George Stephenson, son of the celebrated father, and himself a bridge and railway engineer, surveyed the bridge and found serious faults. He recommended extensive reconstruction as the only alternative to a new bridge. The rebuilt bridge, according to the Sunderland Museum, was opened to traffic on 5 March 1859: the cost was the same as that of the original bridge—£40,000. By 1925 increased traffic so seriously overloaded the bridge that the town built itself a new one, which was opened in 1929.

TWENTY-EIGHT DIFFERENT VIEWS

In the Sunderland Museum collection there are twenty-eight different views of Wearmouth Bridge, all varying in details of the shipping, the figures on the banks of the river, the number of lamp-posts, etc. Of the original bridge of 1796 there are six views from the east, five from the south-east, and twelve from the west. Views of the bridge after the alterations in 1859 comprise four from the east, and one from the west. Many of the specimens are marked: the makers include J. Phillips, Hylton Pottery; Dawson & Co.; Moore & Co.; Dixon & Co.; Scott, Southwick.

The Sunderland Museum's booklet gives a complete description of each view on pieces in its possession, numbering them for reference; a most useful piece of work for which collectors should be grateful.

C. NEWCASTLE

Overshadowed by its neighbour on Wearside, but hardly less important as a source of lustre pottery was the city of Newcastle upon Tyne. As we have seen, one of Sunderland's most important lustre-makers—the Malings—fired their first kiln at Newcastle in 1817 at the height of the early development of lustre ware. In fact by so doing, they seem to have been one of the causes of much Newcastle ware being largely

42

credited to Sunderland, for long after their removal they continued to use the same engravings.

However, the Laing Art Gallery and Museum at Newcastle has now built up a collection of authenticated local ware, and its curator, Mr C. Bernard Stevenson, who made available the picture below and that on page 56, has been able to distinguish features peculiar to the Tyneside potteries.

MALINGS

The Malings built the Ouseburn Bridge Pottery when they moved from Sunderland, and worked it for many years; and in 1853 they built the still existing New Ford Pottery, the only one which still operates on Tyneside, making domestic and specialized industrial earthenware. The factory mark—MALING, or simply M—is occasionally found.

SEWELL & DONKIN

There was a pottery at St Anthony's from about 1780, which in 1804 was acquired by a Mr Sewell who later developed the partnership of Sewell & Donkin. Some very fine-quality lustre ware was made here and exported to the Continent; some of it was creamware of the Staffordshire sort, some the local white ware. There were quintal flower-holders and jugs with cupids and vine leaves in relief, as well as much teaware. Marks include the single word SEWELL and SEWELL & DONKIN.

Pink lustre teapot, by Patterson & Co., Sheriff Hill, Newcastle upon Tyne. (Laing Art Gallery and Museum, Newcastle upon Tyne)

43

THOMAS FELL & CO.

The year 1817 saw the establishment of the St Peter's Pottery by Thomas Fell and Thomas Bell: the concern was known as Thomas Fell & Co. Its marks include FELL & CO with an anchor and a cable; the name FELL associated with the arms of the town; F & CO.; and the single letter F, which has puzzled many collectors.

PATTERSON'S OF SHERIFF HILL

In the Laing Art Gallery's collection there are pieces with the 'cottage' decoration bearing the mark of the Sheriff Hill and Tyne Potteries, originally owned by a George Patterson, who later took on a partner named Ford. The wares bear the marks PATTERSON & CO; TYNE POTTERY; and FORD & PATTERSON, SHERIFF HILL POTTERY. This was a short-lived enterprise, which seems to have come to an end in about 1845. Other Tyneside enterprises which may have been engaged in the making of lustre ware include R. Davies & Co., of the Tyne Main Pottery, and John Carr & Sons, of Low Light Pottery at North Shields.

Newcastle, like Sunderland, had its bridge, again òne of the largest in the world when it was built in 1849. It is over a quarter of a mile long and carries both a railway and a road. Being 112 feet above high-water level it is justly

Leeds dish in silver 'resist', 12½ ins. diameter. Marked LEEDS POTTERY. (Fitzwilliam Museum, Cambridge)

named the High Level Bridge. Views of it are to be found on locally made lustre ware, sometimes in combination with views of the Wearmouth Bridge. Malings were big makers of jugs and mugs bearing this design.

D. LEEDS

The cream-coloured earthenware of Leeds, with its delightful texture and its pierced decoration, its fine transfer printing and its exquisite harmonies of colour painting, has long been an ardent quest of pottery collectors. The factory was founded in Hunslet, then a mile from the centre of the city, some time before 1758, and two brothers named Green who were partners about 1780 were joined by William Hartley to form the business known as Hartley, Green & Co. For the next forty years the enterprise was immensely successful—in 1791 there was a turnover of over £50,000—with a huge export trade to the Continent, where the famous creamware made at Leeds, and also in Staffordshire by Wedgwood and others, was putting the native *faience* out of business.

The success of the firm with its pierced, moulded, and enamelled creamware has overshadowed its work in lustre ware. A very small proportion of this, as with all Leeds pottery, is marked; but in view of the use of the LEEDS

Puzzle jug in 'all-over' silver, with punched ornamentation typical of work in Leeds creamware, 1805–15. (Art Institute of Chicago)

45

POTTERY mark by potters in the town at the end of the nineteenth century, Leeds marks are automatically suspect until proved correct.

CATALOGUES AND DRAWING BOOKS

Fortunately the firm published a range of catalogues giving descriptive lists of the wares in production, and engraved illustrations of them, for the guidance of wholesalers and retailers and also export agents. The first one appeared in 1783, and others in 1785, 1786, 1794, and 1814. There are also extant a series of drawing books, three of which are in the Victoria and Albert Museum; they consist of drawings and designs which have been pasted into old account books of the pottery, and they date from about 1778 to 1793. In the Leeds City Museum and Art Gallery are nine more books showing drawings and designs of the wares dated between 1781 and 1814.'

With the help of these and other special studies it has been possible to compare some of these drawings—which of course were intended for all kinds of decorative techniques as well as lustre ware—with marked examples, and to identify a number of distinctive types. There is, for example, the unmistakable Leeds lion in silver 'resist' on both jugs and dishes, accompanied by conventionalized trees rather in the manner of those in the willow pattern. The stylized floral pattern also appears by itself on other pieces. Then there is a whole range of silver 'resist' jugs with very freely drawn birds, rather in the manner of some of those in enamels. Similar patterns are to be found in purple-pink lustre.

LEEDS PUZZLE JUGS

Another outstanding contribution made by Leeds to lustre ware—and also to an old pottery institution—was the puzzle jug. Everyone will have seen these in one form or another: they have a more or less complicated series of hidden pipes and prior knowledge of the way they work is necessary to drink from them without spilling the liquid over oneself. They are often engraved with some such rhyme as:

> Come, gentlemen, and try your skill,
> I'll hold you sixpence, if you will,
> That you don't drink this liquor all
> Unless you spill or let some fall.

Another version runs:

> Within this jug there is good liquor,
> 'Tis fit for Parson or for Vicar;
> But how to drink and not to spill
> Will try the utmost of your skill.

There seem to have been at least two types made; the smaller round jug derived from a delftware shape of the seventeenth century, and the large jugs on pedestals like the annular jugs made in German stoneware. Both sorts were freely patterned with the Leeds punched decoration.

E. SWANSEA

Swansea is a name better known to collectors of porcelain than pottery. Prices for the delicious soft-pastes made there, and also at Nantgarw under the inspiration of William Billingsley, have soared to fantastic heights in the last few years. Although the material was the equal of the finest Sèvres, its fragility led to serious losses in the kiln, and

Swansea earthenware plate with notched rim, painted in red, brown, and green enamels, having also deep underglaze blue painting, over which are brush strokes of copper lustre.

porcelain was made there for only a very short time; whereas fine earthenware was produced for many years.

CAMBRIAN POTTERY

One first hears of what was to become the Cambrian Pottery about the year 1764, when a William Coles took a lease in the Strand of a site of an old copper works.

The first products made at the pottery were household wares—butter pans, bowls, plates—for local sale, using the native red or buff clays. In 1790 a younger son of Coles took a fresh lease in partnership with George Haynes, an energetic businessman who first seems to have come to Swansea in the brewing trade, his family having been so engaged at Henley-in-Arden in Warwickshire.

They much extended the pottery and began to make fine creamwares on the Staffordshire and Leeds models, also green and yellow glazed wares, and the dry cane wares chiefly associated with Josiah Wedgwood. In view of the inexperience of both partners in making wares of this quality, they must have imported workmen from Staffordshire: they certainly brought in decorators like Thomas Pardoe of Derby and Worcester, and Thomas Rothwell from Hanley. The wares made in the 1790s were often marked SWANSEA impressed or painted in enamels: work decorated by Pardoe is sometimes found marked CAMBRIAN in flowing italics in the painter's own hand. CAMBRIAN POTTERY is also found on pieces of this era, painted in colour over the glaze.

LEWIS WESTON DILLWYN

In 1802 there appeared on the scene a gentleman named Lewis Weston Dillwyn who was to make a considerable mark upon the pottery industry in South Wales. He was neither a potter nor a businessman, but a botanist in his mid-twenties, whose work in that field earned him a Fellowship of the Royal Society: so that in the early years of the partnership it was obviously the older and experienced Haynes who still dominated and controlled the production at Swansea.

After business quarrels with Haynes, Dillwyn took into partnership Timothy and John Bevington. This régime lasted from 1811 to 1817, when the wares were marked DILLWYN & CO, sometimes with the addition of SWANSEA. Having become interested in the manufacture of porcelain, Dillwyn then dissolved his partnership with the Bevingtons, who carried on the pottery on their own account until 1824: they used their name on the wares made during their tenure of the place.

After a failure of both the porcelain factory and the earthenware pottery, Dillwyn moved in again, closed the 'China Works', and being unable to sell the earthenware factory he took it over himself. He also seems to have taken on as agent a John Hancock—perhaps a relative of the man of that name who claimed to have invented the art of using 'gold, silver, and steel' lustres and who spent a few years in Swansea.

Until the year 1831, Lewis Weston Dillwyn remained in control, greatly improving the quality of the product and making many innovations. After that, he handed over to his son Lewis Llewellyn Dillwyn, who managed affairs until 1850, when the pottery was taken over by David Evans, formerly a cashier or manager, and his partner John Evans Glasson, and later by his son D. J. Evans who worked the pottery for another twenty years.

Meanwhile earthenware was being made elsewhere in Swansea. When Dillwyn fell out with Haynes, the latter seems to have started, with an undercover interest which did not affect his covenant not to compete elsewhere in the town, what became known as the Glamorgan Pottery. Some of the wares made there are marked with the initials B.B. & I., or B.B. & CO., after the names of the partners, Baker, Bevans & Irwin. In 1837, however, Dillwyn bought the pottery and closed it down, no doubt to remove competition in a difficult period.

Two years later, however, a William Chambers started to build a pottery at Llanelly and took there some of the workmen from the old Glamorgan Pottery. At first, since Dillwyn still had this establishment's moulds, plates, etc., many of the designs made at this pottery were quite new. The South Wales Pottery, as it was called, did very well, proving a very formidable rival to the Cambrian Pottery, and outlasted all the others, buying up their plant and equipment as they went out of business. The concern continued under various ownerships right down to the year 1927.

'CHAMELEON' LUSTRE

So far as lustre ware is concerned, the first documented Welsh piece seems to be a most interesting mug in the British Museum. It was decorated by Thomas Pardoe in what Mr Nance calls 'chameleon' lustre, with festoons of flowers and diapered ornament in a design reminiscent of Persian pottery. It is marked CAMBRIAN in Pardoe's hand in the same lustre as the decoration. It is in the opaque china, or fine white earthenware, which was being made at the Cambrian Pottery in the late Haynes era—1795–1805. On the base, in ink, are written the words: 'The first piece of chameleon lustre ever made.' This has been authenticated

Sporting jug, silver 'resist' with transfer printing, coloured in blue, brown, and yellow. Staffordshire or Swansea? (Sotheby & Co.)

as the handwriting of Mrs Judith F. Dillwyn Nicholl, sister of Lewis Weston Dillwyn.

The colour of the lustre suggests that it may be a mixture of copper and gold or platinum, and although it looks superficially like the normal metallic lustre, it shows vivid iridescence of the type usually associated with the Hispano-Moresque wares, and later developed by the nineteenth-century potters mentioned on pages 60–1. One wonders whether the iridescence of this lustre is due to the thinness and decay of the metallic film or whether the Swansea pottery was at this early stage experimenting along these lines.

SWANSEA STYLES

There are several other Swansea pieces which seem to date from this era. There is a smaller mug in the Nance bequest at Cardiff which has the 'cottage' decoration in a pink lustre like the 'chameleon' type just mentioned, but darker in tone.

The same colour is also used on jugs and mugs of about 1810 to 1812, in a very free style reminiscent of some delft-ware painting. The jug itself has a moulded pattern with a raised rectangular panel, and smaller heart-shaped ones, with insects and flowers on a ground of lightly impressed dots. Mr Nance traced this unusual style of decoration to a type of eighteenth-century blue and white Chinese porcelain mug which was also in his collection. He shows that this pattern was also used for flower painting by Thomas Pardoe. It was featured at Swansea certainly before 1811 and into the Bevington period. One such mug in the Glynn Vivian Gallery at Swansea has a view painted after a print by Thomas Rothwell.

To this early date, or a little later, belong also two jugs with transfer designs of sporting scenes. Both have Swansea shapes and other characteristics—the glaze, the type of foot and handle—and whereas in one the background is painted with pink lustre similar to that used on the embossed jug mentioned above, the other is in silver lustre. Neither of them is marked—except in one case with workmen's strokes in silver—something seen elsewhere on Swansea wares.

A date is given us by what is known as the Sir John Owen jug, which has a yellow glazed ground with a silver lustre border. An inscription in red overglaze script commemorated the election on 30 October 1812, as M.P. for the County of Pembroke, of John Owen, in a 'contest of Eleven Days against the Honble John Frederick Campbell Esq. and a *Trio* of peers and Created a Baronet Tuesday Novr. 3rd 1812'. It also gives the actual result of the poll. This jug is also unmarked but Mr Nance considered it to be of un-doubted Swansea make.

Silver lustre edges are also to be found on a tea-set with the interesting brown transfer printing which was being made in some quantity in the first Dillwyn era between 1811 and 1817. There is a part tea-set printed in golden brown with groups of shells and seaweed on a creamy-white ground. Here, for once, there *is* a mark impressed—DILLWYN & CO —on the plate, while the cream-jug is from the same mould as was used for making a non-lustred porcelain cream-jug and sucrier bearing Swansea marks.

SWANSEA SWANS
Some pink lustre wares of distinctive types date from after Lewis Weston Dillwyn's return to the pottery. There is a jug painted with a cottage (not exactly *the* 'cottage') and mountain lake and boat landscape; and there are the plates with basketwork borders and pierced rims so familiar to us in creamware, but now in pink lustre with decoration either of the 'church' pattern or loosely painted roses, or of the distinctive swans. These latter are found with the broken circle mark DILLWYN & CO SWANSEA and might be thought to be an exclusively Swansea pattern by way of a rebus, or pun, on the name.

From a later period still come shapes similar to some made

Swansea plate painted in pink lustre with the 'swan' design, green basket weave border and pierced wicker border. Impressed mark DILLWYN AND CO. SWANSEA. C. *1825. 8 ins. diameter.* (Sotheby & Co.)

in the Cymro Stone China (and so marked), which was a rather harder white earthenware developed in the time of Lewis Llewellyn Dillwyn; these too have swiftly drawn roses like those on early salt-glazed ware or delftware. There are marked specimens dated between 1836 and 1847. Plates with copper lustre ornament of flowers and vases painted over underglaze blue bear the Dillwyn mark.

COW MILK-JUGS

Most famous among the lustre wares of Swansea, however, are the cow milk-jugs with mottled lustre. There are two quite distinct types of these—those reared at the Cambrian Pottery, and the others at the Glamorgan. The Cambrian cows have alternate spots of pink and enamel colour, and are often marked with a small impressed D, as the full mark would obviously have been difficult to apply. They seem to belong to the Lewis Weston Dillwyn period: when not so marked they can be compared with those made in the same

Glamorgan Pottery (Swansea) cow milk-jug with pink 'splashed' lustre. (Royal Institution, Swansea)

53

mould but decorated with black transfer patterns of flowers and shells.

At the Glamorgan factory, the cows are quite different around the head and neck, and also in some of the embossed details. They are $5\frac{1}{2}$ ins. high and 7 ins. long, and most of those which survive are transfer printed in black, or occasionally in red or green: they can also be found covered with a brown 'rockingham' glaze. The lustre-painted cows have a highly iridescent purplish-pink lustre with spots left in paler pink or white; the stands are usually painted with green enamel.

COLLECTORS' CAUTION

In general, therefore, it appears that although considerable quantities of lustre wares were made at Swansea, and perhaps also at Llanelly, much of that attributed to the potteries there is still of unproven origin: it could as easily have been made in Staffordshire, or on the north-east coast. This especially applies to the early 'resist' wares such as the famous sporting jugs which were once freely awarded to Wales. With so much of the other Welsh wares marked, it would be difficult to account for so much unmarked 'resist'—why should the potters have discriminated?

So far as 'all-over' lustre is concerned it does not seem that any marked specimens have survived. So here again it is a question of 'not proven'.

But the collector of lustre ware has one great advantage when he comes to identifying the products of South Wales——the painstaking labour of love which the late Mr Nance put into his great work on the wares of Swansea and Nantgarw, and the collection he bequeathed to the National Museum of Wales in Cardiff—so vast that, as with icebergs, only a small proportion can be shown.

By comparison with other documented and identified wares here available, the collector can go a long way towards deciding the claims of Swansea, Sunderland, Newcastle, or Staffordshire for his pieces.

6. Rhyme, Reason, and History

The odd inscriptions on lustre ware are many and varied. They cover an astonishing range of thought, feeling, and emotion; they also commemorate events, landmarks in history, and popular feelings. Their very *naïveté* gives us a most vivid picture of the age and of the everyday thoughts of the people for whom they were written.

A collection of those on Sunderland wares was put together in a booklet by the Sunderland Museum not long ago; and although all these are local products, many of them were used or originated elsewhere, and appear on other kinds of pottery as well. Some obviously hark back to delftware days, others seem to have been taken from poetry books of the day. Some are reasonably well written; many are the merest doggerel. There are verses that are quite affecting; there are others which are totally bawdy. Taking them all in all, they are a branch of folk literature which would well repay further study.

As might be expected from the age, moral admonitions have a large share in the verses. Plaques carry their texts on to the walls, suitably framed in lustre; while love in all its moods also finds expression.

Plate printed in black and decorated in 'splashed' pink lustre; probably made at the Garrison Pottery, Sunderland. (Sunderland Museum)

Election mug, transfer printing in black with pink lustre.
(Laing Art Gallery and Museum, Newcastle upon Tyne)
Text plaque, with border in 'splashed' pink lustre, imitating a picture frame.

Many of the verses deal with parting, as one might expect from pottery made in a seaport.

TRADE AND POLITICS

In times when good trade meant food, and bad trade meant desperate hardship and privation, many were the hopes expressed for prosperity:

> Success to the Fleece
> To the Plough and the Sail.
> May our Taxes Grow Less
> And our Commerce ne'er Fail.

The coal trade is wished success; so are the fishermen and the farmers.

Heroism has already been noted on the jugs, mugs, and teapots referring to Jack Crawford, the hero of Camperdown, but patriotism runs all the way through these pieces.

Masonic inscriptions abound, as on other types of earthenware, while humour, gentle or boisterous, is to be found here, even irony:

> Always speak the truth
> But not at all times the whole truth.

It took a courageous husband to have the following on his punch bowl:

> From rocks and sands
> And barren lands
> Kind fortune keep me free
> And from great guns and women's tongues
> Good Lord deliver me.

COMMEMORATIVE

Events and persons are commemorated on lustre ware from all the centres. Ships of all kinds are here—from Nelson's *Victory* and the whole fleet at the Battle of the Nile, the famous steamship *Great Eastern* and clipper ships and yachts. A transfer print of British and French flags supported by sailors and used on bowls, jugs, and mugs marks the Crimean War with the verse:

> May they ever be united
> Vive L'Empereur
> God Save the Queen.

The famous 'Ascent of the Aerial Balloon' is shown on some pieces, in one case with the patriotic but perhaps rather irrelevant, 'Producing the bark to tan the hide off Buonaparte'.

Heraldry is of the popular sort, such as the Mariners Arms, the Farmers Arms—with nicely displayed forks and other farming gear. There are also the arms of the Ancient Order of Foresters, and the Loyal Independent Order of Oddfellows.

BOXERS

Prize-fighters were popular, as on other pottery. The earliest of the celebrated fights to be commemorated were those between Tom Cribb, Champion of England, and Tom Molineaux, the American Negro. The lustre potters seem also to have marked the fights between Spring and Langan, the Irish champion. Some plaques and jugs illustrating

57

Boxers: Tom Cribb, Champion of England v. Tom Molineaux, the Negro from Virginia, challenger.

these events have been noted with the maker's mark, John Aynsley, an engraver at Lane End, in the Potteries. Another famous fighter of the time who is so commemorated is Daniel Donnelly, also an Irish champion.

AMERICAN HISTORICAL

Just as the War of Independence of 1776 interrupted a thriving export trade in pottery from England to the United States, so too did the one which broke out between the two countries in 1812. And in the same way that Josiah Wedgwood, Josiah Spode, John Turner, and many another Staffordshire potter, made haste to celebrate the heroes of the newly independent Republic rather than their own, so in this new war did they commemorate the American victories.

Like the creamware which had been a staple export in the pre-war years, these pieces were well potted; they were mainly jugs of the usual Staffordshire shapes, mostly with the high neck. The engravings, one on either side, were printed in black, puce, or brick-red. The tankards or mugs usually carried one engraving, perhaps a portrait.

Among the ships depicted on these wares, the most frequently met with is the celebrated frigate the *Constitution*, which seems to have won the war almost on her own.

Other American naval heroes who appear on the pottery include Commodore Stephen Decatur, who commanded the frigate *United States*, and captured the British *Macedonian*. There was also Captain James Lawrence, who earned imperishable fame when he was in command of the *Chesapeake* in her deadly battle with the British cruiser *Shannon*.

Washington and Benjamin Franklin appear on the jugs, and there is a whole series commemorating the visit of the French General Lafayette to America in 1824: sometimes this is associated with an engraving of the surrender of General Cornwallis in 1781, the official end of the War of Independence.

Many of these engravings were made by a firm called Bentley, Ware & Bourne, of Shelton, using either original drawings from America or copies of prints in books published there.

ANTI-SLAVERY

In the early days of lustre ware, anti-slavery was a popular cause in England as well as in America. Conspicuous among the pieces marking this feeling is an engraving bearing the same theme as the famous Wedgwood jasper ware medallion shown in another book in this series (WEDGWOOD), where a slave is kneeling in chains and there is an inscription 'AM I NOT A MAN AND A BROTHER'. The medallion became the seal of the Slave Emancipation Society.

American Commemorative, 1812–14. (Below right) *Black printing with silver 'resist' decoration, and the American eagle on the reverse.*
(Below left) *Captain Stephen Decatur, of the frigate* United States.
(Right) *American Eagle Jug.* (Henry Francis du Pont, Winterthur Collection)

7. Iridescent Lustre

Standing quite apart from the lustre wares we have so far been looking at are those which aim, not at the reproduction of metallic effects, but at iridescence, shimmering and changing colour in the light.

For the origin of this type of lustre one has to go back to the wares of the Persians or Mesopotamians in the tenth century, specimens of which have been found in Spain. It may be these which inspired the Moorish potters at Malaga and Valencia and Aragon to produce the superb Hispano-Moresque wares, glowing with splendid fires of golden, greenish, or tarnished copper. Similar pieces are being produced at Manisses in Valencia to this day.

VALENCIAN WARES

The earliest of them are attributed to Malaga, made by the Moorish potters up to the reconquest of the province by the Spaniards. But in the next hundred years there developed the beautiful Valencian wares made by Moorish workmen. Not a great deal of the common wares have survived. What we have are the more splendid pieces, the great armorial dishes, the bowls painted with sailing-ships, the noble heraldic animals, birds, and figures.

From Valencia, along with the other wares which were to become known as *maiolica* (after the Majorcan ports through which the wares were exported), the lustre wares went to Italy and there inspired the painters of Deruta and Gubbio to try their hand at the art of lustre. They produced a ruby-red and golden yellow; also bluish and mother-of-pearl lustre effects, then greatly prized by buyers all over Europe.

In the nineteenth century, a number of potters seem to have started work again almost simultaneously on the problem of iridescence. There was Cantegalli in Florence,

Massier in France, Zsolnay in Hungary. In England there was that remarkable character William de Morgan, and a little later the band of artists, chemists, and craftsmen who worked under the Burtons for the art pottery founded by the Pilkington's Tile Company near Manchester.

WILLIAM DE MORGAN

This artist-potter, a friend of William Morris and Edward Burne-Jones, seems to have rediscovered the art of iridescent lustring without benefit of the contemporary work being done in Europe. In about 1874 he found a clue in the way the yellow stain of silver on glass shows iridescence when over-fired; and in a small gas-fired muffle he found that both copper and silver gave a lustre when the gas was damped down so as to penetrate the muffle.

After what he described as an 'interruption'—he set his house on fire and burned the roof off—he developed his process in Chelsea. He seems to have achieved the effects of the medieval lustres by putting sawdust or wooden chips into the kiln at the right moment to achieve the reducing atmosphere.

There was a strong ruby-red from copper; and a yellowish grey from silver oxide which could give a bluish-silver iridescence. He painted a great many tiles, large flat dishes

Hispano-Moresque dish of buff earthenware, painted in iridescent yellow lustre and blue Valencia. Fifteenth century. 17 ins. diameter. (Victoria & Albert Museum)

and vessels, usually on a plain white glazed ground, but sometimes on a blue. His themes were usually animals, real and mythical, ships, birds, or fish, all conceived in flat patterns of great boldness, with flowing lines admirably adapted to the shapes he used.

ROYAL LANCASTRIAN

In his book *Royal Lancastrian Pottery, 1900–1938* Abraham Lomax, who was a chemist at the Pilkington works for many years, described the problems the lustre-makers had in reviving the old iridescent technique. As he explains it, the method at the Lancastrian Pottery involved painting on the already fired glaze a compound of silver and/or copper diluted with clay or some other inert material, made suitable for the artist's brush with some oily medium; then firing the ware in a specially constructed kiln. At what was called a cherry-red heat, the atmosphere in the kiln was changed from an oxidizing to a reducing one by restricting the supply of air.

Only silver and copper have proved suitable metals for iridescence—the platinum used by the early-nineteenth-century men is unsuitable since it does not tarnish. But a great deal is still a matter of guesswork: Mr Lomax himself, after a lifetime spent in studying the problem, can still only guess at the reasons for some of the failures—and the brilliant successes.

PILKINGTON ARTISTS

Chief among the Pilkington artists, and in fact one of the great figures in modern English ceramics, was Gordon M.

Tin-glazed earthenware vase, designed by William de Morgan and painted in iridescent lustre by Jim Hersey, c. 1890. (Victoria & Albert Museum)

Forsyth, who was in charge of the art department at the Lancastrian Pottery and later left to become Superintendent of Art Instruction in Stoke-on-Trent.

Another Lancastrian artist, Richard Joyce, worked on designs by the famous Walter Crane. Others who were responsible for lustre painting in the early years of this century included William S. Mycock, who painted lustre wares for thirty of his forty years at Pilkington's, mainly producing conventional floral designs and geometric patterns. Richard Joyce, a brilliant painter of animal, bird, and fish designs admirably adapted to the forms of the vessels, showed at the Exhibition of 1908. Charles E. Cundall, who afterwards achieved fame as a portrait painter and became an R.A., was another painter of lustre ware at Pilkingtons, and so too was Gwladys M. Rogers, who was excellent at heraldic animals.

Collectors of Lancastrian pottery find the task of identification made easier by the system of marking used after 1904. Not only was the name or monogram of the firm (usually PL) incorporated in the piece, but also that of the designer. There were other marks showing the artist's personal monograms, usually easily recognized as they were based on initials.

(Right) *Earthenware vase, painted in iridescent ruby lustre, after a design by Walter Crane. Maw & Co., Benthall, 1899.* (Victoria & Albert Museum)

Royal Lancastrian semi-porcelain bowl, painted in brown and gold iridescent lustre with an inscription in white glaze. About 1920. Designed by Gordon Forsyth, and bearing his monogram 'GF'. Royal Lancastrian Pottery. (Victoria & Albert Museum)

A highly distinctive type of lustre ware was produced in Shropshire by Maw & Co., once celebrated for their tiles. They developed a whole series of tiles, and were particularly interested in the coloured glazed wares which the Victorians called 'majolica'. Soon afterwards the firm moved to a pottery at Benthall, near Broseley, where in the late eighteenth century the Thursfields had been making wares similar to those of near-by Jackfield, the name of which village stands now for any pottery where a black glaze is used over red earthenware.

The work that Maw & Co. carried out there in architectural ceramics—tiles, tesserae for mosaics, etc.—is still to be found in buildings of the era: but they also developed a line of art pottery wares, using the services of famous designers like Walter Crane. The picture on page 63 shows an example of the ruby lustre work which they were turning out at about the end of the century.

BERNARD MOORE

Bernard Moore, whose beautiful glazed wares made in emulation of the great Ming monochromes are now collectors' pieces, was another potter who interested himself in experimenting with the original iridescent lustre ware. Moore came from a Longton potting family, and in 1870, together with his brother, took over his father's china business. Although domestic wares continued to be produced the pottery moved more and more in the direction of decorative pieces. In about 1905 the works closed down, and Moore devoted himself entirely to designing and consultancy work. Between then and 1914 he employed a number of well-known artists who, like those of the Lancastrian Pottery, signed their work with their initials—the master potter's name, or initials, was also used.

ALFRED AND LOUISE POWELL

At Wedgwood's some interesting work with iridescent lustre

was done by Alfred H. Powell, who died in 1960 at the age of ninety-five. His wife was Louise Lessore, grand-daughter of Emile Lessore, one of the famous Wedgwood artists in the late nineteenth century. Powell was a member of the so-called Cotswold school of artist-craftsmen—Ernest Gimson's furniture was another expression of its work. He combined the artistic outlook of the William Morris school with natural skill and taste as a designer, and with his wife founded a school of freehand women painters at Etruria before the First World War. Some of their work was in the lush foliate designs beloved of the William Morris school, some used formal patterns from the early days of Etruria, or restrained patterns of the sprigged New Hall type. The Powells themselves, and also their daughter Thérèse, who later married the painter Walter Richard Sickert, did some admirable personal pieces.

The tradition established by the Powells in the freehand painting department was carried on by Miss Millicent Taplin, whose floral patterns with silver lustre were popular for many years.

A number of smaller potteries tried their hands at iridescent lustre, notably the one established by Sir Edmund Elton at his home at Clevedon Court, Somerset. One of his

Modern metallic lustre ware in the early-nineteenth-century tradition. Lustre decorated jugs by Josiah Wedgwood & Sons Ltd, in the twentieth century, but no longer in production. With the modern Wedgwood marks. (Josiah Wedgwood & Sons Ltd)

specialities was a lustre glaze with a crackled effect, as on Chinese porcelain.

But the lustre pottery made in recent years has for the most part reverted to the traditional English metallic type. The silver and gold 'all-over' lustre tea and other wares which are being sold in the china shops at present have already been mentioned. Earlier in this century, Wedgwood's made lustre jugs of the type shown on page 65 although these lines have now been discontinued. Their current production includes some very pleasant jugs decorated in purple lustre with one of the firm's admirable foliate designs, which they seem to be able to adapt in each generation without losing the distinctive Wedgwood touch.

Actually in production at the moment by the Stoke firm now known as Portmeirion Potteries Ltd are jugs which are straight reproductions of older types in museums and private collections, and are not intended in any way as fakes. They bear the maker's mark, and of course are in a modern body which could never be mistaken for anything produced in the early days. Nevertheless, collectors should be warned that cases have been reported where the mark has been removed and the wares offered as genuine old pieces.

One hopes that by now the reader will have picked up enough hints to enable him to guard against these hazards. First, as shown on page 20, he must acquaint himself with the touch and look and feel of the china or earthenware bodies used; then study the lustre glazes themselves, comparing genuinely old with genuinely new—remembering that lustre wares can always be re-lustred. After that, study the other decoration and the forms, comparing always with other contemporary wares. Last of all, look at the marks— if there are any!

WITHDRAWN
LIBRARY USE ONLY